PARES SCALES

For Individual Study
and Like-Instrument Class Instruction

by GABRIEL PARÈS

Revised and Edited by Harvey S. Whistler

Published for:

Flute or Piccolo . . . . Parès-Whistler

Clarinet . . . . Parès-Whistler

Oboe . . . . Parès-Whistler

Bassoon . . . . Parès-Whistler

Saxophone . . . . Parès-Whistler

Cornet, Trumpet or Baritone 𝄞 . . . . Parès-Whistler

French Horn, E♭ Alto or Mellophone . . . . Parès-Whistler

● Trombone or Baritone 𝄢 . . . . Parès-Whistler

E♭ Bass (Tuba - Sousaphone) . . . . Parès-Whistler

BB♭ Bass (Tuba - Sousaphone) . . . . Parès-Whistler

Marimba, Xylophone or Vibes . . . . Parès-Whistler-Jolliff

For Individual Study and Like-Instrument Class Instruction
(Not Playable by Bands or by Mixed-Instruments)

RUBANK®

HAL•LEONARD®
CORPORATION

7777 W BLUEMOUND RD PO BOX 13819 MILWAUKEE, WI 53213

Key of C Major
Long Tones to Strengthen Lips

Also practice holding each tone for EIGHT counts.

When playing long tones, practice (1) ⟨⟩ and (2) ⟨⟩.

Embouchure Studies

Slur as many tones as possible.

Slur as many tones as possible.

Key of F Major
Long Tones to Strengthen Lips

Scale of F

11

Also practice holding each tone for EIGHT counts.

When playing long tones, practice (1) ⦏⟨ and (2) ⟨⟩

12

13

14

15

16

Embouchure Studies

Slur as many tones as possible.

Key of G Major
Long Tones to Strengthen Lips

Also practice holding each tone for EIGHT counts.

When playing long tones, practice (1) ——◁ and (2) ◁——▷.

24

25

26

Embouchure Studies

Slur as many tones as possible.

Slur as many tones as possible.

Key of B♭ Major
Long Tones to Strengthen Lips

31 Scale of B♭ (5) (9) (13)

Also practice holding each tone for **EIGHT** counts.

When playing long tones, practice (1) ⬦⬦ and (2) ⬦⬦.

35

36

Embouchure Studies

Slur as many tones as possible.

Slur as many tones as possible.

Key of D Major
Long Tones to Strengthen Lips

41 Scale of D (5) (9) (13)

Also practice holding each tone for EIGHT counts.

When playing long tones, practice (1) ⟍ and (2) ⟍⟋.

42 (5) (9) (13) (17)

43 (5) (9)

Embouchure Studies

Slur as many tones as possible.

Slur as many tones as possible.

Key of E♭ Major
Long Tones to Strengthen Lips

Also practice holding each tone for EIGHT counts.

When playing long tones, practice (1) ⟨ and (2) ⟨ ⟩.

55

56

57

Embouchure Studies

Slur as many tones as possible.

Slur as many tones as possible.

Key of A Major
Long Tones to Strengthen Lips

62 Scale of A

Also practice holding each tone for EIGHT counts.

When playing long tones, practice (1) ⧽ and (2) ⧼⧽.

66

67

Embouchure Studies

Slur as many tones as possible.

Slur as many tones as possible.

Key of A♭ Major
Long Tones to Strengthen Lips

Also practice holding each tone for EIGHT counts.

When playing long tones, practice (1) ⸺ and (2) ⸺

76

77

78

79

Embouchure Studies

Slur as many tones as possible.

80

Slur as many tones as possible.

81

Key of Db Major
Long Tones to Strengthen Lips

Also practice holding each tone for EIGHT counts.

When playing long tones, practice (1) and (2)

86

87

Embouchure Studies

Slur as many tones as possible.

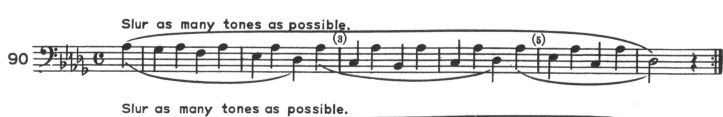

Slur as many tones as possible.

Key of A Minor
(Relative to the Key of C Major)

Long Tones to Strengthen Lips

Scale of A Harmonic Minor

Scale of A Melodic Minor

Also practice holding each tone for EIGHT counts.

When playing long tones, practice (1) and (2)

Embouchure Studies

Slur as many tones as possible.

Slur as many tones as possible.

Key of D Minor
(Relative to the Key of F Major)
Long Tones to Strengthen Lips

Scale of D Harmonic Minor

Scale of D Melodic Minor

Also practice holding each tone for EIGHT counts.

When playing long tones, practice (1) and (2)

Embouchure Studies

Slur as many tones as possible.

Slur as many tones as possible.

Key of E Minor
(Relative to the Key of G Major)
Long Tones to Strengthen Lips

Scale of E Harmonic Minor

Scale of E Melodic Minor

Also practice holding each tone for EIGHT counts.

When playing long tones, practice (1) ⟨ and (2) ⟩.

Embouchure Studies

Slur as many tones as possible.

Slur as many tones as possible.

Key of G Minor
(Relative to the Key of Bb Major)
Long Tones to Strengthen Lips

Also practice holding each tone for EIGHT counts.

When playing long tones, practice (1) ⎯⎯< and (2) ⎯⎯<⎯⎯.

Embouchure Studies

Slur as many tones as possible.

Slur as many tones as possible.

Key of B Minor
(Relative to the Key of D Major)
Long Tones to Strengthen Lips

Scale of B Harmonic Minor

116

Scale of B Melodic Minor

117

Also practice holding each tone for EIGHT counts.

When playing long tones, practice (1) and (2) .

118

119

Embouchure Studies
Slur as many tones as possible.

120

Slur as many tones as possible.

121

Key of C Minor

(Relative to the Key of E♭ Major)

Long Tones to Strengthen Lips

Also practice holding each tone for EIGHT counts.

When playing long tones, practice (1) ⟨ and (2) ⟨⟩.

Embouchure Studies

Slur as many tones as possible.

Slur as many tones as possible.

Key of F# Minor

(Relative to the Key of A Major)

Long Tones to Strengthen Lips

Also practice holding each tone for EIGHT counts.

When playing long tones, practice (1) ⟨ and (2) ⟨⟩

Embouchure Studies

Slur as many tones as possible.

Slur as many tones as possible.

Key of F Minor
(Relative to the Key of A♭ Major)
Long Tones to Strengthen Lips

Scale of F Harmonic Minor

134

Scale of F Melodic Minor

135

Also practice holding each tone for EIGHT counts.

When playing long tones, practice (1) ⟨ and (2) ⟩.

136

137

Embouchure Studies

Slur as many tones as possible.

138

Slur as many tones as possible.

139

Key of Bb Minor
(Relative to the Key of Db Minor)
Long Tones to Strengthen Lips

Scale of Bb Harmonic Minor

Scale of Bb Melodic Minor

Also practice holding each tone for EIGHT counts.

When playing long tones, practice (1) ⏤◁ and (2) ◁▷.

Embouchure Studies

Slur as many tones as possible.

Slur as many tones as possible.

Major Scales

The following scales are NOT to be
slurred on the TROMBONE. The slurred
markings are for BARITONE only.

Harmonic Minor Scales

Melodic Minor Scales

The following scales are NOT to be slurred on the TROMBONE. The slurred markings are for BARITONE only.

Arpeggios

The following Arpeggios are NOT to be slurred on the TROMBONE. The slurred markings are for BARITONE only.

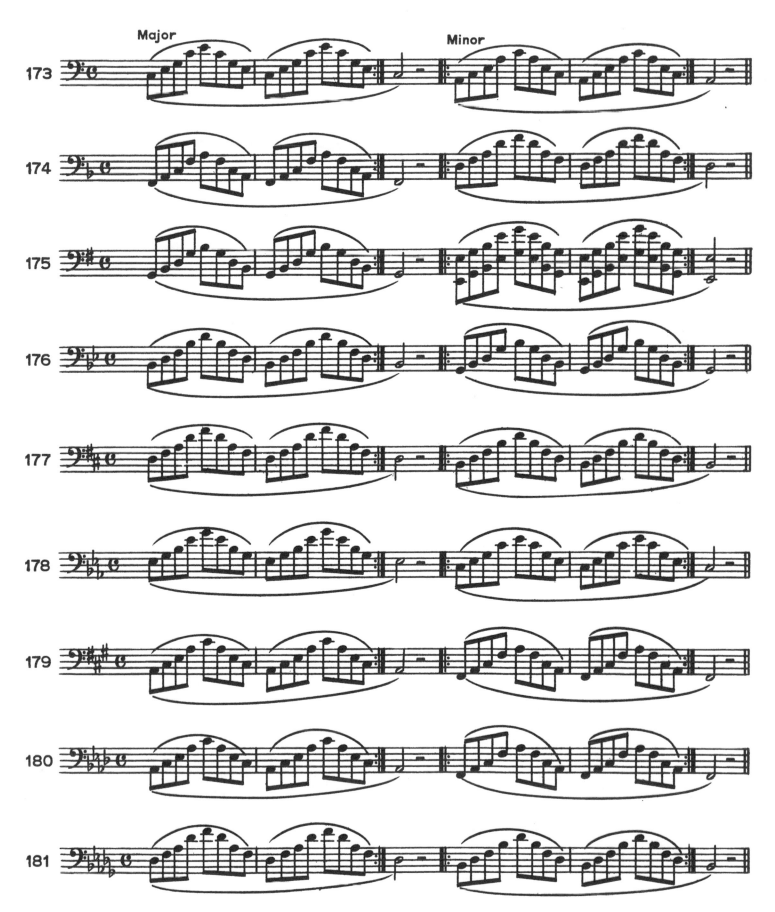

Chromatic Exercises

The following chromatic exercises are **NOT** to be slurred on the **TROMBONE**. The slurred markings are for **BARITONE** only.

Chromatic Scales in Triplets

Chromatic Exercises

Chromatic Study in Triplets

✱ This tone (A♯ or B♭) may be produced on the trombone by playing in an artificial 8th position, and blowing the pitch flat at the same time. Such a procedure, however, should be carried out only when executing rapid passages.

Lip Slurs

44

Lip Slurs

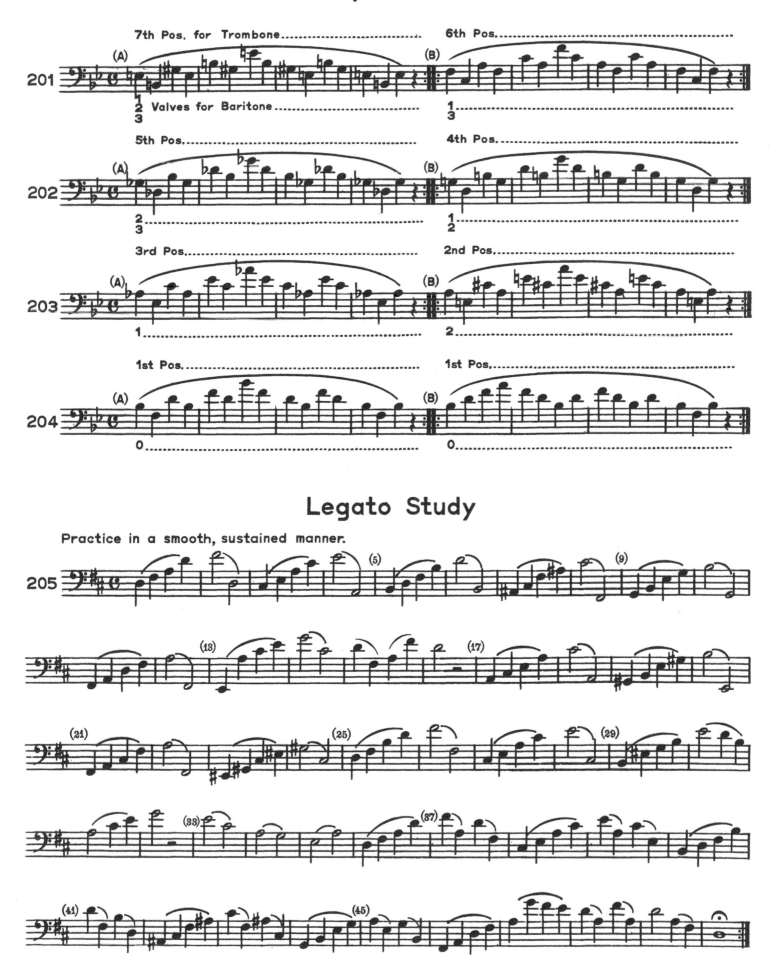

Legato Study

Practice in a smooth, sustained manner.

Technic Builder

Velocity Study

Artist Etude

Octave Study No. 1

Octave Study No. 2